YESHUA IS
ישוע
THE NAME
יהוה

The **Important Restoration**
of the **True Name** of the **Messiah!**

DOMINIQUAE
BIERMAN, PHD

Yeshua Is The Name © 2007-2021 by Dominique Bierman.
All rights reserved.

This book may not be copied or reprinted for commercial gain or profit. The use of short quotations or occasional page copying for personal or group study is permitted and encouraged. Permission will be granted upon request.

Unless otherwise identified, Scripture quotations are from the: New American Standard Bible – NASB. Used by permission. All rights reserved.

Words such as Jesus, Christ, Lord, and God have been changed by the author, back to their original Hebrew renderings: Yeshua, Messiah, Yah, Yahveh, and Elohim, respectively.

First Printing March 2007, Second Printing June 2021

Paperback ISBN: 978-1-953502-55-1
E-Book ISBN: 978-1-953502-56-8

Published by Zions Gospel Press | shalom@zionsgospel.com
52 Tuscan Way, Ste 202-412
St. Augustine, FL, 32092, USA

Kad-Esh MAP Ministries | www.kad-esh.org | info@kad-esh.org

This book is dedicated to the Messiah, Yeshua Himself, with all my love and devotion.

"Let this mind be in you which was also in Messiah Yeshua, who, being in the form of Elohim, did not consider it robbery to be equal with Elohim, but made Himself of no reputation, taking the form of a bondservant, and coming in the likeness of men. And being found in appearance as a man, He humbled Himself and became obedient to the point of death, even the death of the cross. Therefore Elohim also has highly exalted Him and given Him the name which is above every name, that at the name of YESHUA every knee should bow, of those in heaven, and of those on earth, and of those under the earth, and that every tongue should confess that Yeshua Messiah is Lord, to the glory of Elohim the Father"

PHILIPPIANS 2:5-11

CONTENTS

Terminology 1

What's the Big Deal? 5

He Will Be Called Yeshua 11

The Name Matters 17

The Lord's Exile Has Ended 21

The Power of His Name 27

His Name is Forever 33

Revocation of the Council of Nicaea 39

Extra Information 47

INTRODUCTION

TERMINOLOGY

Before you begin to read this book, I would like you to be familiar with some renewed terminology that will help your understanding. In any new move of God, there is new, or renewed terminology introduced. It is no different in the case of this End time move of restoration. Here are four terms which are used throughout the entire book. I would like you to be familiar with:

YAHVEH

Yahveh is the name of the Lord as revealed to Moses and used throughout the prophetic writings. *Yahveh* means the "I AM" and the "Ever-Present God."

This name is often used in conjunction with the name; *Elohim*, which is the name of the "Creator God."

YAHVEH ELOHIM

The I AM who is the Creator. The short way of saying Yahveh is Yah as in Halelu-Yah. So, many times I will use the Word Yah instead of "God."

THE TORAH

Torah is the Hebrew word for "instruction in righteousness," commonly called Law.

In this book, Torah only refers to the Law of Yahveh in the Five Books of Moses and Law throughout the Bible. In this book, the Torah does not apply to rabbinical laws or manmade traditions. In a place where I mention a rabbinical tradition, I will refer to it as such.

The Torah includes three types of charges:
- Commandments
- Statutes or Judgments
- Laws or Precepts

> Because that Abraham obeyed My voice, and kept My charge, My commandments, My statutes, and My laws.
>
> Genesis 26:5

Notice that before Moses was given the Torah at Mount Sinai, Abraham already walked and obeyed the Torah. Abraham already followed the Torah since the Torah of the Living YAH (God) is eternal.

Notice that before Moses was given the Torah at Mount Sinai, Abraham already walked and obeyed the Torah. Abraham already followed the Torah since the Torah of the Living Yah (God) is eternal.

- The Commandments are eternal (referring to the Ten Commandments).

- The Statutes are also eternal and connected with holiness and worship. Note: following the Statutes connected with Temple Worship requires more background knowledge. Since we are now the Temple of the Holy Spirit, an interpretation from the Holy Spirit is needed about how to follow them today.
- The precepts are eternal principles, though the actual instructions were temporary and only relevant to the issues of the times they were given. So, today, we keep the principles and apply them to our times. As we walk with the Holy Spirit of Yah, He continues to give us precepts daily!

Here is the ticket to lifelong success and prosperity:

This Book of the Law (Torah) shall not depart from your mouth, but you shall meditate in it day and night, that you may observe to do according to all that is written in it. For then you will make your way prosperous, and then you will have good success.

Joshua 1:8

Abraham, who is the father of the faith, understood and walked in the way which he had been given. Also in these End times, the Torah is being restored: a revelation by the Holy Spirit to the church. As we meditate in Yah's holy Commandments, judgments and precepts; the Word will become flesh in us and will produce the fruit of obedience. This obedience will make us blessed, successful, and prosperous.

YESHUA

Yeshua (commonly called Jesus Christ) is the real Hebrew name for the Jewish Messiah. In Hebrew, Yeshua means "salvation, deliverance and redemption." Throughout this book, I will use His Hebrew name only.

Yeshua is the Torah made flesh or the Living Torah. As you follow Him, and His *Ruach HaKodesh* (Holy Spirit) He will lead you to the Truth.

And you shall know the truth, and the truth shall make you *free*.

John 8:32

CHAPTER ONE

WHAT IS THE BIG DEAL?

"Therefore repent and return, so that your sins may be wiped away, in order that times of refreshing may come from the presence of Yahveh; and that He may send Yeshua, the Messiah appointed for you, whom heaven must receive until the period of restoration of all things about which Elohim spoke by the mouth of His holy prophets from ancient time."

ACTS 3:19-21

It is as simple as the above verses: Yeshua will not return until all things are restored. Among the "all things," one of the most important ones, if not the *most* important one, is the restoration of His Holy name. His true name was lost due to replacement theology that was established as Church Doctrine at the time of the Council of Nicaea. This Council divorced the Church from everything Jewish and from the true Jewish name of the Messiah as well. Before the return of Yeshua, all things will be restored, which includes the Jewishness of the Faith in Messiah and the name of Messiah as well. Since He was not born Greek but Jewish, His identity as a Jew as well as His original and eternal name are an extremely important part of this *urgent* end time restoration of all things.

This is no light matter, and therefore, the Creator commands us to *repent* before all things can be restored. In my previous books (see list at the end of the book), I have led the Ecclesia ("Church") in repentance since 1996 for harboring replacement theology, pagan feasts, lawlessness (Torahlessness), and AntiMesitojuz (Anti Messiah-Israel-Torah-Jewish- Zionist) in any way, shape, or form. Now it is time to *repent* for calling Him by any other name but His true name. Repent means to turn around and go back to Yah's (God) ways, forsaking our own sinful ways, including the doctrines of demons and men.

There is absolutely no scripture that endorses the change, translation, or transliteration of His name. Rather, to the contrary, there is more than enough scriptural evidence for His name to remain intact and honored *as is*. Replacement theologians changed His name to Jesus Christ, and their doctrine must be discarded if we are to please the Father. Failing to repent about this issue will demonstrate a serious breaking of the *first* Commandment,

> "And you shall love Yahveh your Elohim with all your heart, with all your soul, with all your mind, and with all your strength. This is the first commandment"
>
> Mark 12:30 NKJV

If we love Him with *all* of our beings, we will be willing to repent and change our ways to His ways. It is no problem when you truly love Him to discard any and all doctrines, (of demons and men) and to burn all of your traditional "sacred cows." If you believe that this is "too radical" wait until you meet the Jewish Messiah in person! All the "sweet" Christian doctrines will fall to the ground and will be burnt to a crisp by the fierceness of His appearance.

"And in the middle of the lamp stands I saw one like a son of man, clothed in a robe reaching to the feet, and girded across His chest with a golden sash. His head and His hair were white like white wool, like snow; and His eyes were like a flame of fire. His feet were like burnished bronze, when it has been made to glow in a furnace, and His voice was like the sound of many waters. In His right hand He held seven stars, and out of His mouth came a sharp two-edged sword; and His face was like the sun shining in its strength. When I saw Him, I fell at His feet like a dead man and He placed His right hand on me, saying, "Do not be afraid; I am the first and the last"

Revelation 1:13-17

He has not called us to *religion* but to *obedience* to His Laws and Commandments. Any time that we honor *tradition* or *people* more than we honor Him we become idolaters. He is sanctifying His Bride and sanctification is only possible through *truth,*

> "Sanctify them in the truth; Your word is truth."
>
> John 17:17

If you love *truth*, you love Him. The name Jesus Christ is *not* His *true* name. If you love Him, you will love His *true* name, Yeshua, and will call Him by His name. If you love popularity with men more than with Him, it is a snare to you! The *fear of man* is a snare! I know great ministers who know the truth about the name of Yeshua and fail to implement it for fear of people's reactions. This is a snare and another type of *idolatry*. Please do not call it "wisdom!"

For the wisdom of this world is foolishness before God, for it is written, "He is *the one who catches the wise in their craftiness.*"

> 1 Corinthians 3:19

A few years ago, I had the privilege of guiding a Bishop from Ecuador on one of my training tours in the Holy Land of Israel. The man was so extremely touched by Yahveh that he went back full of passion to implement all that he had learned. He went to the director of his denomination and told him about the Jewish Roots of the faith and all about the Name. He asked the President: "Do you know what the *true* name of the Messiah is?" The man answered, "Yes, I know, it is *Yeshua*". The astonished Bishop asked him, "Why then did you not teach us this *truth*?" The President answered, "because it is not *popular*!" He ordered the Bishop not to talk about it to his congregants, nor to implement anything of what he had learned! Praise Yah that this precious Bishop is a true Servant of the Most High and displayed no fear of man. A while later he was expelled from his denomination as he *refused* to forsake the *truth*.

"The fear of man brings a snare, but he who trusts in Yahveh will be exalted."

Proverbs 29:25

What about you? Are you the reader a *true* Servant of *Yah* or do you care more about popularity? If so, you need to *repent*! Judgment has already begun in the House of God! All things will become restored and Yeshua will return. The sooner, the better!

"For it is time for judgment to begin with the household of Elohim; and if it begins with us first, what will be the outcome for those who do not obey the gospel of Elohim? *And if it is with difficulty that the righteous is saved, what will become of the godless man and the sinner?* Therefore, those also who suffer according to the will of Elohim shall entrust their souls to a faithful Creator in doing what is right."

1 Peter 4:17-19

Many believers know that the true name of the Messiah is Yeshua but they do not understand the life and death importance of repenting and restoring His Holy name. This book will give you the understanding and then the *choice* will be yours:
Whether to please *man* or *Yahveh*.

1

CHAPTER TWO

HE WILL BE CALLED YESHUA

"She will bear a Son; and you shall call His name Yeshua, for He will save His people from their sins." Now all this took place to fulfill what was spoken by the Lord through the prophet"
MATTHEW 1:21-22

When the Angel Gabriel visited Yeshua's mother, Miriam, she was a young Jewish virgin in Nazareth. The Angel then visited Joseph, her betrothed, and revealed to him the Holy Name of the Holy Child in Miriam's womb. The Angel said His name shall be *Yeshua* for He will *save* His people from their sins. This is about the salvation of Israel, His people! They will not be saved in any other name but in His *true name*. Satan knows this so he has enticed the Church to *change* this name into a Greek one with pagan roots. It has *no* Hebrew meaning at all and certainly does not mean *salvation*. It is derived from the Greek god Zeus, and other derivatives of that same god, like Iaso or Iesu.

In the book "Come Out of Her My People" by C.J. Koster, we find an excellent and thorough research about the roots of the name of Jesus or Iesous. Though Koster (not being a Jew or a Hebrew Scholar) misses it on the right Hebrew spelling and pronunciation of the name of Messiah his research from the Greek about the name of Jesus is very revealing.

"In spite of attempts made to justify the "translating" of the Father's Name and His Son's Name, the fact remains: A personal name cannot be translated! It is simply not done. The name of every single person on this earth remains the same in all languages. Nobody would make a fool of himself by calling Giuseppe Verdi by another name, Joseph Green, even though Giuseppe means Joseph and Verdi means Green. Satan's name is the same in all languages. He has seen to it that his name has been left unmolested!

However, let us further investigate the names Ieso (Iaso) and Iesous. According to ancient Greek religions, Apollo, their great Sun-deity, had a son by the name of Asclepius, the deity of healing, but also identified with the Sun. This Asclepius had daughters, and one of them was Iaso (Iwso), the Greek goddess of healing. Because of her father's and grandfather's identities as Sun-deities, she too is in the same family of Sun-deities. Therefore the name Iesous, which is derived from Ieso, can be traced back to Sun-worship.

We find other related names, all of them variants of the same name Iasus, Iasion, Iasius, in ancient Greek religion, as being sons of Zeus. Even in India we find a similar name Issa or Issi, as surnames for their deity Shiva. Quite a few scholars have remarked on the similarity between the names of the Indian Issa or Issi, the Egyptian Isis and the Greek Iaso.

In our research on the deity Isis we made two startling discoveries. The one was that the son of Isis was called Isu by some. However, the second discovery yielded even further light: The learned scholar of Egyptian religion, Hans Bonnet, reveals to us in his Real lexikon der agyptischen Religionsgeschichte, p. 326, that the name of Isis appears in the hieroglyphic inscriptions as ESU or ES. No wonder it has been remarked, "Between Isis and Jesus as names confusion could arise. Isis also had a child, which was called Isu by some. This Isu or Esu sound exactly like 'Jesu' that we find the Saviour called in the translated Scriptures of many languages, e.g. many African languages." ("Come Out of Her My People" by C.J. Koster page 63)

Yeshua was not born a Gentile. He was born a Jew, into the Covenant with Israel and into the Hebrew language, the language of the Scriptures! This revelation alone should be enough for any noble believer to repent and to restore the Holy name of Yeshua. In fact, my book should end here! However, I will continue, in order to remove any possibility of *doubt*!

One of the most ludicrous arguments I have sadly heard, quite often is, "It says Jesus in my Bible and the Bible is infallible." I have even heard this from *pastors*! It is time for us to *think*! The New Covenant portion of the Bible was written in Hebrew and/or Greek. The Angel appeared to Joseph who was a Jewish man. In what language do you suppose Gabriel spoke to Joseph? In Hebrew of course! What name do you think that He gave him for the Holy Child? Well, the Hebrew name of course which means *salvation*, for He will *save* His people from their sins.

"She will bear a Son; and you shall call His name Yeshua, for He will save His people from their sins." Now all this took place to fulfill what was spoken by the Lord through the prophet"

Matthew 1:21-22

That is the name *Yeshua* which in Hebrew means salvation from the Hebrew root word *Yeshia*. All Hebrew words have a *three* letter *root*.

ישע ישוע

Jesus is Greek and it does not mean salvation! The *given name* was Hebrew and it means *salvation*! No one has the *right* to change the name given by Elohim Himself through His Angel Gabriel. Yahveh is the Father, and He named His Son! How would you like someone to *change* the name of your son that you have named? Imagine how the Father *feels* about the change of the *holy name of his son*?! He is definitely not happy about this. He has put up with it because of the *ignorance* of men but now He *commands all* people to *repent*!

Another very sad argument I have heard is this one:

"Well, let's not make a 'fuss' about this and let us not be 'religious' about the name!"

In the 21st century many Christians have mistaken *holiness*, *righteousness* and *truth* for religiosity. The condition of most churches in the area of *holiness* is distressing! In the name of "freedom" sin is allowed to run rampant. It is seldom, *if ever*, truly corrected by the modern-day pastor. In many congregations throughout the USA, and other places, a "seeker friendly" mentality has been instilled. The modern church doesn't want to "ruffle any feathers" and is going further and further away from the Messiah Himself. The "gospel" has become quite irrelevant, and many do not even want to hear the name of Jesus Christ as they feel hostile towards it.

One day I was shopping in a health foods market in Dallas, Texas. I was in the line to pay as I saw the man in front of me trying to "witness" to the cashier. She was a young lady, tattooed from top to bottom. Some of the tattoos were very demonic including dragons, pentagrams and snakes. As she heard the name of "Jesus Christ" she stiffened and hardened her heart, refusing to listen. When it was my turn to pay, I said to her, "I would like to follow up on what the young man was saying to you except I would like to tell you the *real* name of Jesus. He is Jewish, was born in Israel, and His *true name* is *Yeshua*. It means salvation, deliverance and healing!" The lady relaxed and sighed a sigh *of relief* as she said, "Thank you, that *sounds much better*!"

Is the Holy Name of *Yeshua sounding much better to you*?

Or will it take the heathen to come in to teach the Christians that *Yeshua* is the *true name* and that it is *time* to *restore it*?

Therefore Elohim also has highly exalted Him and given Him the name which is above every name, that at the name of

Yeshua every knee should bow, of those in heaven, and of those on earth, and of those under the earth, and that every tongue should confess that Yeshua Messiah is Lord, to the glory of Elohim.

Philippians 2:9-11

CHAPTER THREE

THE NAME MATTERS

"Nothing will be attempted if all possible obstacles must first be removed."

SAMUEL JOHNSON

I must confess that when I began to understand the importance of the restoration of Yeshua's name I was a bit reluctant to make a fuss about it. I had enough on my "plate" already with trying to restore the Body of Yeshua to Torah, Holiness and the Biblical Feasts. In fact, I had "the hutspah" (nerve) to say to the Almighty, "When you stop answering prayers in the name of Jesus then I will address the subject of Your Name with the Church." I am amazed sometimes at how kind he is with our foolishness! Who am I to tell Him? The next service that I preached at I found myself preaching *vehemently* about the *importance* of the restoration of

His Holy Name. That was a few years ago! Right now, I feel that this *is urgent* and that we can make no more excuses about it! **He wants to *return ASAP* and *all* things must be restored!**

I began to do my own bit of research into this. Since He confirms His Word with signs, wonders and miracles I began to *test* it and *every* time I did, He answered with miraculous healing, deliverance and/or salvation. I believe that very soon you will realize that your prayers in the name of Jesus do not have enough power to cast out the end time demons. I realized this when I was ministering in a congregational meeting in Chiba, Japan in January of 2006! I was at the end of the meeting; the ministry team was ministering deliverance to a Filipino lady.

She was raving and screaming and was not getting free at all. This went on for quite some time, with the ministry team screaming, "in the name of Jesus Christ come out!" The lady apparently had been some sort of Christian who had backslidden. After some time of playing this "game," when I thought that the devil had had enough "fun," I asked them *to stop* and to bring her to me. I told her to be *quiet* and to look into my eyes: "Now, just repeat after me, *Yeshua*." "*Yeshua*," she said, and as she repeated His Holy, *powerful*, eternal name she began *to jump* with *joy*. She screamed and wept in brokenness! "Yeshua, Yeshua my Lord, my Savior, I love you, I love you, this is the *true* name, the name of the Messiah!" Needless to say, the devil left in a jiffy and the lady was *free*! That was quite a demonstration of the importance of the restoration of His Holy name! Later on, I will mention some others that I have witnessed.

Important Disclaimer

Am I saying here that He has not answered to the name of *Jesus*? If that is what you think you are wrong! I believe that many people have been saved in the name of Jesus and that many have been healed and delivered in the Greek name! However, many have also been persecuted, tortured and murdered in the name of Jesus Christ. The entire Genocide of the Jewish people from the Council of Nicaea, throughout the Dark Ages, the Crusades, the Spanish Inquisition, and the Nazi Shoa (Holocaust) have happened in the name of Jesus Christ! They began the expulsion of Jews in Germany by raising up the Cross and Jesus Christ on it declaring *Juden Raus* - or "Jews out" because you killed Jesus Christ. Countless numbers of people, mostly Jewish, but also native indigenous African and even Moslem tribes will *not respond* to the name of Jesus Christ, which has been used to hurt and murder their people!

He wants His Holy name restored *now*! The name of Yeshua has been kept *intact* for such a time as this! There are no memories of killing or destruction in the beautiful name of Yeshua, Praise be to *Yah*! (God) Yahveh is the name of the Father and it means:

I Am

Not "I was" or "I will be"! He is the *I Am* and is *now* doing a *new* (renewed) thing. He is restoring all things, including Yeshua's Name. If you reject this restoration, it is not me whom you are rejecting but Him. I am only His agent as it is His idea! When He was restoring *tongues* and *healing* many people opposed the move and consequently died spiritually. They also thought that it was OK to stay living in the *past*. **But it is never OK to stay in past ignorance.** When the cloud of glory (like Israel's in the Sinai Desert) moves, we need to *move* with it. If not, you will die in the spiritual desert of past experiences and of religion!

"Behold, the former things have come to pass, now I declare new things; Before they spring forth I proclaim them to you."

Isaiah 42:9

CHAPTER FOUR

THE EXILE OF THE LORD HAS ENDED

"On your walls, O Jerusalem, I have appointed watchmen; All day and all night they will never keep silent You who remind Yahveh, take no rest for yourselves; And give Him no rest until He establishes And makes Jerusalem a praise in the earth."

ISAIAH 62:6-7

One day I was walking and praying on the walls of Jerusalem with a ministry team who has answered the call of Isaiah 62:6-7.

"On your walls, O Jerusalem, I have appointed watchmen; All day and all night they will never keep silent You who remind Yahveh, take no rest for yourselves; And give Him no rest until He establishes And makes Jerusalem a praise in the earth."

Isaiah 62:6-7

As we were praying, the leader shared with me the following: "The Church must understand that *Yeshua* made Alyah and He is now back in His own Land."

To "make Alyah" means to return and go up to Zion. This is the term for the Jewish people who return to their homeland, after 2000 years of painful exile. I made Alyah 36 years ago from Chile and many Jews have returned from all over the world. "*Jesus*" of course is Jewish, so He also has to *return* to His own land! What this brother really meant is that the Church needs to change her focus from *Rome* to *Jerusalem*. Christianity as we know it today was born in Rome under the Roman Empire. It was the Eastern Roman Emperor Constantine who instituted the religion of Christianity, divorced from the Jews and anything Jewish. (See appendix at the end of the book, "Revocation of the Council of Nicaea.")

It is in this context that the Greek name of the Messiah was institutionalized, and the *original* Hebrew Name *forbidden*. As The Body of the Lord is called "back home" to a Jerusalem based faith and to the original Gospel made in Zion; to restore the original and only true foundations of

Faith which are Jewish, so is she called to restore the original name of Messiah to her lips. It was customary in ancient times for the pagan rulers to change the names of prominent Jews who were living in *exile*. This happened to Joseph and to Daniel, who became known as Belteshazzar and also the three Hebrew lads Mishael, Azariah and Chananyah who became Meshach, Shedrach and Abednego. These new names were the pagan names of foreign gods. That was how they honored those prominent Jews who displayed the Power of the Most High God. Their Holy Hebrew names were changed. In the same way, when Yeshua was in *exile* after the destruction of the Temple in Jerusalem in year 70 AD and the Jewish believers were scattered throughout the Roman Empire, the heathen who were beginning to believe in Him looked for a name that would please the masses and would demonstrate how important He was. They found no other than *Iesous*, which etymologically carries the name of great Greek gods. In the case of Joseph, his name was changed to that of an Egyptian god and Yoseph (Joseph) married the daughter of the pagan priest.

> "Then Pharaoh named Joseph Zaphenath-paneah; and he gave him Asenath, the daughter of Potiphera priest of On, as his wife. And Joseph went forth over the land of Egypt."
>
> Genesis 41:45

Everyone in Egypt, including his own wife, called him Zaphenath-paneah. He definitely answered to that name. However, this only went on until the time that *all things were restored*. When His brothers came to him, his name became **Yoseph** again! After his family was restored to him, he became Yoseph again and even Pharaoh called him Yoseph (there is no **J** in the Hebrew language! Thus, it is Yoseph and not Joseph)! This was the *fullness* of time for Yoseph's dream to come to pass. In the same way, now is the fullness of time for Yeshua's dream to come to pass, when His Jewish family will recognize Him and bow down before Him!

The *first* thing that Yoseph did in order to reveal himself to his brothers was to *say* his *true name*! Until that moment he had been introduced as the Egyptian Ruler, Zaphnatpaanah and his brothers had not recognized him! Likewise, the Jewish people will not recognize their Brother and Messiah when He is introduced as Jesus Christ the Christian God.

> "Then Yoseph could not control himself before all those who stood by him, and he cried, "Have everyone go out from me." So there was no man with him when Yoseph made himself known to his brothers. He wept so loudly that the Egyptians heard it, and the household of Pharaoh heard of it. Then Yoseph said to his brothers, "I am Yoseph! Is my father still alive?" But his brothers could not answer him, for they were dismayed at his presence."
>
> Genesis 45:1-3

Yeshua is in Heaven right now, but His Bride is on the earth. The only way that He can reveal Himself to Israel is through a circumcised (of heart) Bride that displays the Jewishness of the Gospel and carries the Name of *Yeshua* and not Jesus Christ!

If you think that I am "Judaizing" you right now, you'd better think again. What god are you serving? What gospel are you preaching? What Bible are you reading? If it is not a Jewish Messiah, a Jewish Gospel and a Jewish Bible, then you are in deception and replacement theology has been your religion (please see Appendix at the end of the book). You'd better *repent* right now as He is coming for a Bride, Pure and Holy who is a Spiritual Jew:

"And he carried me away in the Spirit to a great and high mountain, and showed me the holy city, Jerusalem, coming down out of heaven from Elohim, having the glory of Elohim Her brilliance was like a very costly stone, as a stone of crystal-clear jasper. It had a great and high wall, with twelve gates, and at the gates twelve angels; and names were written on them, which are the names of the twelve tribes of the sons of Israel. There were three gates on the east and three gates on the north and three gates on the south and three gates on the west. And the wall of the city had twelve foundation stones, and on them were the twelve names of the twelve apostles of the Lamb."

Revelation 21:10-14

The New Jerusalem has 12 Foundation Stones which are the twelve *Jewish Apostles* of the Lamb. It has twelve gates and they are the twelve *tribes of Israel*. The Lamb Himself is a Lion; a Jewish Lion:

"...and one of the elders said to me, "Stop weeping; behold, the Lion that is from the tribe of Judah, the Root of David, has overcome so as to open the book and its seven seals."

Revelation 5:5

His brothers, the Jews, are getting saved again. Israel is established again and the time for the nations is coming to a *close* when *all* Israel will be saved.

For I do not want you, brethren, to be uninformed of this mystery, so that you will not be wise in your own estimation, that a partial hardening has happened to Israel until the fullness of the Gentiles has come in; and so all Israel will be saved; just as it is written, "The Deliverer will come from Zion, he will remove ungodliness from Jacob." "This is My covenant with them, when I take away their sins."

Romans 11:25-27

The Messiah is *Jewish* His Gospel is *a Jewish* based Gospel, and His Name is *Jewish* and it is: *Yeshua*. Period.

You are probably asking yourself, is it "sinful" to call Him Jesus Christ now that I know His *real name*? My answer is, why would you want to keep on calling Him by a pagan name now that you know better?

"It will come about in that day," declares Yahveh, "That you will call Me Ishi And will no longer call Me Baali." For I will remove the names of the Baals from her mouth, so that they will be mentioned by their names no more."

Hosea 2:16,17

Most of the names of Greek gods are some sort of derivative of the god "Baal" which means Master. In old times, the Israelis used to call Yahveh by foreign names thinking that they were worshipping Him. One of the most beautiful signs of forgiveness and restoration is *Yah's* desire to have an intimate relationship with us as a *husband*. In Hebrew, the word *ishi* is *my husband*! This is possible through Yeshua who is our *ishi*. When we call Him Jesus Christ, we are still calling Him Baali, the Greek name with pagan roots. In Israel today people are so far from Him that they use the name *baal* to say husband. It is very rare for someone to use the name *ishi* for their husband. The sign of *forgiveness* and *mercy* is the restoration of *intimacy* with our Heavenly Bridegroom who is our *ishi* through His Holy Name *Yeshua*!

Why would anyone get offended about this? The *true* Bride of Messiah gets delighted at being able to call Him *ishi- Yeshua* again! Call Him by His Name right now and enjoy His very intimate sweet presence. *Try it now*! He will confirm His Word with signs following!

"Come Yeshua, Ishi, and reveal yourself to me through Your Holy Name."

CHAPTER FIVE

THE POWER OF HIS NAME

"And my message and my preaching were not in persuasive words of wisdom, but in demonstration of the Spirit and of power,"
1 CORINTHIANS 2:4

The restoration of His name will bring about great *revival*, salvation, healing and deliverance for many people groups who have been closed to the Gospel. I saw the power of evangelizing in the name of Yeshua when Yah sent me and my team to the city of Cuzco, in Peru, where the ruins of Machupichu are. The city is in a very remote area and sits on a very high mountain. 99.9% of the population are staunch Catholics. I was establishing a work in Lima, Peru, when the Father spoke to me, telling me to fly to Cuzco. As I was preparing to leave, some well-meaning Christians warned me that there is no way to evangelize in Cuzco as they reject all missionaries and are completely closed to the Gospel. I thanked these precious saints and told them that there is no place too hard when it is the Almighty who sends you and we left.

As I was on the way it dawned on me that most of these Catholics had gone to this remote place during the Spanish Inquisition. Peru had a terrible Inquisition and all the Jewish Converts to Catholicism were in danger at that time. In fact, in the Inquisition Museum in Lima, it says that over 80% of those murdered during the Inquisition in Peru were Jewish! I thought to myself that those Jews who converted to Catholicism to escape death probably decided to go as far away as possible from the watchful eye of the inquisitors in Lima. What better place than the remote and very hard to access Cuzco? If this was the case, then they would be totally closed to the Gospel of Jesus Christ but totally open to the Gospel of Yeshua HaMashiach! I was going to "experiment" with the name!

Upon our arrival to the Cuzco airport, we met a man who was in charge of a tourism booth. We purchased some train tickets from him to go up and visit the very interesting ruins of Machupichu. We ended up befriending him. As we talked about spiritual matters he became highly interested and joined us for a walk to show us around the town. When it came to the pertinent question, "Would you like to know *real* name of Jesus Christ?," his eyes immediately lit up with expectation as he nodded in the affirmative. I said, "It is in Hebrew as He is a Jew". "It is Yeshua HaMashiach and it means salvation, healing and deliverance." He repeated the name, savoring every letter as his eyes filled with tears. "Do you want to accept Him?" I asked, to which he nodded emphatically. I led him in a prayer of salvation, and he was born again! It was that easy! He immediately proceeded to ask me pertinent questions about idolatry and the need to forsake it. The *true* fruit of the new birth is an immediate desire to forsake all sin!

I have had a few powerful experiences with the name of Yeshua among the Catholics. A few years ago, I was preaching in David Herzog's Passover Glory Conference when my brother, who is one of the most anointed evangelists of our time, gave an altar call. When no-one seemed to be moving as the name of Jesus Christ was mentioned I felt that it was time to "use the Name." I said, "Come and be saved by Yeshua, the Jewish Messiah. He loves you and is waiting for you..." All of a sudden, from the left-hand side of the hall, an entire group of people rose up as *one* and began to run to the altar. They were *all* Catholics! What a glorious harvest we had that day! But they only responded when the name of Yeshua was mentioned!

Another time I was in Peru where my disciples there blessed me with a massage at a country club. As I was lying on the massage table, anticipating a relaxing time, which I "sorely" needed, the masseuse began to tell me about all of her experiences with the Virgin! Oy vey! And I wanted to relax! She told me how many candles she had lit and how many prayers she had prayed. On and on she went. I prayed under my breath in tongues, and finally, after half an hour of her "unloading" I asked her this simple question. "Do you want to know the *true* Hebrew name of Jesus Christ, from Israel?" She answered like a surprised little girl, with, "Yes, please!" I said, "it is *Yeshua* and it means salvation, healing and deliverance." The response was glorious! For the next half an hour she muttered the name of Yeshua as she continued to massage me! She must have said His name over a hundred times! When the massage ended, I looked into her eyes and asked her if she wanted to accept Yeshua? As she said *yes*, I led her in a prayer of renunciation of all idolatry. She was instantly filled with the Holy Spirit, praying in glorious tongues! This was the *best* massage I had ever had!

Not long ago I was in the Philippines teaching about the importance of restoring the true name of the Messiah. I said, "Bring me anyone here who is sick. I won't pray for them but just decree the Holy Name of Yeshua and He will demonstrate the power of His Name." They brought me a deaf and dumb lady and I just decreed *Yeshua*! Her ears opened up immediately and for the first time ever she could hear. She began to worship Yeshua right away!

These kinds of instant miracles and healings, by simply declaring His name in order to demonstrate the importance of restoring it, are becoming the norm. I believe that they will increase into amazing signs and wonders. His Holy Hebrew name has been kept secret and untainted for such a time as this. This is His most powerful end time weapon! I want to reiterate here that all these miracles happened in the context of my preaching, teaching and revealing His name, and they are a direct corroboration of this subject! He loves to confirm His Word with signs following!

> "And on the basis of faith in His name, it is the name of Yeshua which has strengthened this man whom you see and know;

and the faith which comes through Him has given him this perfect health in the presence of you all."

Acts 3:16

In John 17:6 Yeshua says that He had "manifested His name." In other words, He had demonstrated the meaning and power of His name. He had *lived up to His name* when He healed the sick, cast out devils, opened blind eyes, fed the multitudes. His name meaning *salvation* in Hebrew includes:

1. Salvation from sin
2. Salvation from sickness
3. Salvation from enemies (including demons!)
4. Salvation from poverty

He demonstrated all of the fullness of His name in His earthly ministry and then He left us His name so we could do the same!

"These signs will accompany those who have believed: in 'My name' they will cast out demons, they will speak with new tongues; they will pick up serpents, and if they drink any deadly poison, it will not hurt them; they will lay hands on the sick, and they will recover."

Mark 16:17-18

CHAPTER SIX

HIS NAME IS FOREVER

*Then Moses said to Elohim, "Behold, I am going to the sons of Israel, and I will say to them, 'The Elohim of your fathers has sent me to you.' Now they may say to me, 'What is His name?' What shall I say to them?" Elohim said to Moses, "I AM WHO I AM"; and He said, "Thus you shall say to the sons of Israel, 'I AM has sent me to you.'" Elohim, furthermore, said to Moses, "Thus you shall say to the sons of Israel, 'Yahveh, the Elohim of your fathers, the Elohim of Abraham, the Elohim of Isaac, and the Elohim of Jacob, has sent me to you,' **This is My name forever, and this is My memorial-name to all generations.***

Exodus 3:13-1

The name of the Father is **Yahveh** and it was revealed for the first time to Moses. Yahveh is the name under which the People of Israel were delivered from slavery; the name under which the Egyptians were smitten, and the Red Sea opened up! This is a mighty powerful name! He said that this is His name *forever* and a *memorial-name for all* generations! In other words, it should not be changed or tampered with and it certainly should not be forgotten! Christians for the most part do not know this name as they call Him by the generic term Lord which is not a name but a title. It can be used for any Master, including Satan! The Jews, for the most part, are so afraid to take His name in vain that they call Him "Hashem," which means "the Name." However, both groups are missing the point here and thus the power of His Holy name! He said:

This is my name forever.

Do not call me by any other name or titles. Do not translate or transliterate!

Memorial-name to all generations.

I want to be *remembered* by My name, not My title!

It is time to call the Father by His name, *Yahveh*. His name carries His power and His authority. It is as awesome as He is!

In Psalm 91, we are told of a great reward for those who know His name:

Because he has loved Me, therefore I will deliver him; I will set him securely on high, because he has known My name. "He will call upon Me, and I will answer him; I will be with him in trouble; I will rescue him and honor him. "With a long life I will satisfy him and let him see My salvation."

Psalms 91:14-16

There is a direct correlation between *loving* Yahveh and *knowing* His name! And the list of blessings for knowing His true name is quite impressive!

1. I will deliver you
2. I will set you securely *on high*
3. I will answer you
4. I will be with you in trouble I will rescue you
5. I will honor you
6. I will satisfy you with long (prosperous) life!
7. I will demonstrate and perform My salvation (Yeshua!) to you

Knowing the name of Yahveh eventually leads us to know and experience the *fullness* of *Yeshua*, the Hebrew word for salvation! It will lead to a revelation of the fullness of His anointed salvation, of His good plans towards us.

In the same way that He is jealous about His own name and does not want it changed, watered down or forgotten, He is also jealous about His Son's name! Like Father like Son! He sent the Angel Gabriel to give a specific name to Joseph that would carry the *purpose* of His coming which was *salvation*. When that name is declared, all the powers and the principalities tremble. They are so deathly afraid of His *true* name that Satan has done his best to conceal it and to encourage its change through transliteration into other names. Names which do *not* mean *salvation* anymore and therefore lack power. Elohim created everything by the Power of His Word. One word created *light*, being *yehi or*! each word in Genesis One created its own meaning, thus the word declared *light* released the *light.* When the word for *trees* was declared it released *trees* into existence and when *Adam* was declared it released *Adam* into existence. In the same way when the name *Yeshua* is declared it *releases salvation (Yeshua* in Hebrew) into existence. It has the power to create the reality of the name into existence!

> Then Elohim said, "Let there be light"; and there was light.
>
> Genesis 1:3

The power of death and life is in the tongue so you can create any atmosphere for good or bad and any reality by using words or using the tongue!

> "Death and life are in the power of the tongue, and those who love it will eat its fruit."
>
> Proverbs 18:21

Decreeing things with your mouth can establish realities. This is the power of words!

> "You will also decree a thing, and it will be established for you; and light will shine on your ways."
>
> Job 22:28

That is why the Scriptures tell us again and again that the ones who call on the *name* of Yahveh will be saved. Yahveh gave the name to His Son, and His name is *salvation (Yeshua).* He is *salvation Himself*
and there is no other name given to men in which to be saved!

"And there is salvation in no one else; for there is no other name under heaven that has been given among men by which we must be saved."

Acts 4:12

There is *no* salvation *or no Yeshua* in any other name and there *is no* other name given to men, not even the transliterated ones. Remember that Jesus is *not* a translation. If it had been a translation, then you would have called Him *salvation and not* Jesus! He has heard prayers and saved many people thus far in His transliterated name, but He will not return until *all* things are restored, especially His Holy name!

"Therefore repent and return, so that your sins may be wiped away, in order that times of refreshing may come from the presence of Yahveh; and that He may send Yeshua, the Messiah appointed for you, whom heaven must receive until the period of restoration of all things about which Elohim spoke by the mouth of His holy prophets from ancient time."

Acts 3:19-21

Now in the context of all that you have read thus far why would you want to call Him by any other name but by His name *Yeshua*?

Therefore Elohim also has highly exalted Him and given Him the name which is above every name, that at the name of YESHUA every knee should bow, of those in heaven, and of those on earth, and of those under the earth, and that every tongue should confess that Yeshua the Messiah is Lord, to the glory of Elohim the Father."

Philippians 2:9-11

A Life Changing Prayer

Thank you, Father, for restoring to me, the true name of Your Son. Dear Yeshua, I recaeive Your Holy name back! Manifest Your name to me in all of its fullness. Amen.

Now begin to worship Him with His Holy name. Repeat it a few times and savor its meaning: salvation, healing and deliverance. Decree it into your life, your family and your finances...

Let there *be Yeshua*!!!

CHAPTER 7

REVOCATION OF THE COUNCIL OF NICAEA

Thus says the LORD, "Stand by the ways and see and ask for the ancient paths, Where the good way is, and walk in it; And you will find rest for your souls. But they said, 'We will not walk in it.'"

JEREMIAH 6:16

The Council of Nicaea solidified the identity theft of the Jewish Messiah into a Roman Christ. I have chosen to expose its lies that have caused much anti-Semitism and the loss of the Covenant and birth name of Yeshua. Renouncing the lies of this council will bring untold deliverance and restoration to the original faith as brought by the Jewish apostles of the Lamb about 2,000 years ago.

From the letter of the Emperor (Constantine) to all those not present at the council. (Found in *Eusebius, Vita Const.*, Lib III 18-20)

When the question relative to the sacred festival of Easter arose, it was universally thought that it would be convenient that all should keep the feast on one day; for what could be more beautiful and more desirable than to see this festival, through which we receive the hope of immortality, celebrated by all with one accord and in the same manner? It was declared to be particularly unworthy for this, the holiest of festivals, to follow the customs (the calculation) of the Jews who had soiled their hands with the most fearful of crimes, and whose minds were blinded. In rejecting their custom we may transmit to our descendants the legitimate mode of celebrating Easter; which we have observed from the time of the Savior's passion (according to the day of the week).

We ought not therefore to have anything in common with the Jew, for the Savior has shown us another way; our worship following a more legitimate and more convenient course (the order of the days of the week: And consequently in unanimously adopting this mode, we desire, dearest brethren, to separate ourselves from the detestable company of the Jew. For it is truly shameful for us to hear them boast that without their direction we could not keep this feast. How can they be in the right, they who, after the death of the Savior, have no longer been led by reason but by wild violence, as their delusion may urge them? They do not possess the truth in this Easter question, for in their blindness and repugnance to all improvements they frequently celebrate two Passovers in the same year. We could not imitate those who are openly in error.

How, then, could we follow these Jews who are most certainly blinded by error? For to celebrate a Passover twice in one year, is totally inadmissible.

But even if this were not so it would still be your duty not to tarnish your soul by communication with such wicked people (the Jews). You should consider not only that the number of churches in these provinces make a majority, but also that it is right to demand what our reason approves, and that we should have nothing in common with the Jews.[1]

Exposing the Lies and Doctrinal Errors of the First Council of Nicaea of 325 C.E.

1. "When the question relative to the sacred festival of Easter…"

The truth: sacred to pagan traditions, this is a pagan name derived from the goddess Ishtar. (Exodus 20:3 and Hosea 2:17.)

2. "…arose, it was universally…"

The truth: Everyone in the universe? Is Constantine the king of the universe? (Isaiah 14:3.)

3. "…thought that it would be convenient…"

The truth: God does not call us to convenience but obedience. (John 15:10.)

4. "…that all should keep the feast on one day; for what could be more beautiful and more desirable than to see this festival, through which we receive the hope of immortality, celebrated by all with one accord and in the same manner?...."

---

[1] Dr. Henry R. Percival's *The Nicaean and post Nicaean Fathers*, Vol. XIV Grand Rapid: Eerdmans pub. 1979, pgs. 54-55

The truth: Without Jews? John 17:21, unity between Jew and Gentile brings the salvation of all mankind. (Psalms 133 and Isaiah 56.)

5. "...It was declared to be particularly unworthy..."

The truth: Yahveh's choice of dates is "unworthy" to Constantine as he sets himself above God's choosing of timings. (Daniel 7:25 and Isaiah 14:13 [Lucifer.])

6. "...for this, the holiest of festivals to follow the customs (the calculation) of the Jews..."

The truth: Which are the original and true calculations? (Leviticus 23:1 and Jeremiah 31:31–34.)

7. "...who had soiled their hands with the most fearful of crimes, and whose minds were blinded..."

The truth: In John 10:17–18 Yeshua lays His own life down (See also John 3:16.) The accusation that "the Jews killed Christ" has been the incentive for the extermination of millions of Jews from that point onwards and until this day, including the Holocaust. (See Matthew 7:17–20, [the fruit of this theology.])

8. "...In rejecting their custom..."

The truth: which is God's custom according to His Word.

9. "...we may transmit to our descendants the legitimate..."

The truth: according to Constantine but not according to the Word of God. (Matthew 26:2, Leviticus 23:1–4, Genesis 1:14, John 20:1–9, Matthew 12:39)

10. "...mode of celebrating Easter which we have observed..."

The truth: pagan name and feast not mentioned in the Holy Scriptures.

11. "We ought not therefore to have anything in common with the Jew, for the Savior has shown us another way"

The truth: Yeshua is Jewish, so if nothing is in common with the Jews, nothing is in common with the Messiah. (Matthew 1, John 19;19, Luke 1:59, Luke 2:21)

12. "our worship following a more legitimate and more convenient course, the order of the days of the week"

The truth: Constantine legitimizes his own ideas in order to gain political power and control and he attempts to dethrone the Word of God on this subject - setting himself and his opinions above Yah and His unchanging Word.

13. "...And consequently in unanimously..."

The truth: without the Jews from which salvation comes! John 4:22

14. "...adopting this mode, we desire, dearest brethren to separate ourselves from the detestable company of the Jew For it is truly shameful for us to hear them boast that without their direction we could not keep this feast. How can they be in the right, they who, after the death of the Savior..."

The truth: Romans 11:15–20 warns the Gentiles not to be arrogant against the Jews or Gentiles will be cut of the Olive tree!

15. "...have no longer been led by reason..."

The truth: true sons of God are not led by reason or Greek philosophy but by the Spirit of God. Since Constantine and the Council of Nicaea, the church in its vast majority has been led by reason and by theologians instead of by powerful apostles. (Romans 8:14, Ephesians 2:20) - these are all Jewish

16. "but by wild violence, as their delusion may urge them"
The truth: What wild violence is he talking about? Unsupported accusation used many times to incite the masses against the Jews like in the Protocols of the Elders of Zion?

17. "They do not possess the truth in this Easter question, for in their blindness and [15th lie] repugnance to all improvements"
The truth: traditions of demons and men that make null and void the Word of God (Matthew 15:3,4, Mark 7:13)

18. "they frequently celebrate two Passovers in the same year. We could not imitate those who are openly in error. How, then, could we follow these Jews who are most certainly blinded by error?"
The truth: Is following the biblical customs error? Who is really blinded here? Gentiles are supposed to be grafted into Israel's Olive tree and not vice versa! (Romans 11:15–20)

19. "For to celebrate a Passover twice in one year is totally inadmissible."
The truth: 2 Chronicles 30:1–3, it is totally scriptural.

20. "But even if this were not so it would still be your duty not to tarnish your soul by communication with such wicked people (the Jews)."
The truth: In other words, Constantine's purpose is to separate from the Jews and the Torah no matter what! Why? 1 John 4:1–3

states that the spirit of anti-Messiah, in operation through Constantine, removes the identity of Messiah as a Jew, and sets himself above God and His Word and His sovereign choice of choosing the Jews to bring salvation.

21. "You should consider not only that the number of churches in these provinces make a majority"

The truth: God has never worked with "majorities" but with obedience. Trusting in the arm of the flesh or the opinions of men brings about a curse! (Deuteronomy 28:1–14, Jeremiah 17:5, Judges 7:2–8, 1 Samuel 14:6)

22. "...but also that it is right to demand what our reason approves..."

The truth: Human reasoning? (1 Corinthians 1:27, Isaiah 29:14b)

23. "...and that we should have nothing in common with the Jews."

The truth: or with the Jewish Messiah or His salvation - John 4:22, Romans 11:15–20. He set the Gentile part of the church onto a path of self-destruction, remaining a wild olive instead of being grafted into the cultivated Olive tree - which is Israel - because of arrogance, removing the foundations of the Jewish apostles and prophets. (Psalms 11:3, Ephesians 2:20, Revelation 21:14)

Prayer Renouncing the First Council of Nicaea of 325 CE

Please pray this prayer. You can copy it to pass it on, and please let us know of your decision. Pray this declaration out loud:

Before the Almighty God of Israel, I stand at this moment to renounce the First Council of Nicaea as led by Constantine. I renounce its foundation and all the anti-Jewish fruit that came out of it from my life. I renounce every doctrinal error and every lie in it, including Replacement Theology in all of its aspects.

I now affirm my faith in YAHVEH, the God of Israel; who is the Creator of the Universe and my Father through the atoning death of His Holy Son Yeshua, who is both the promised Jewish Messiah and God in the flesh. Right now, I affirm my faith in the resurrection of Yeshua the Messiah and the outpouring of the Holy Spirit from the Day of Shavuot (Pentecost) and onwards, to all that repent and believe in the Son. I hereby affirm my belief that I'm grafted into the Olive tree that represents Israel, and together with the believing Jewish people, I will inherit eternal life. I at this moment affirm that the God of Israel will never forsake His people, neither will He forget His covenant with the Jews or with the Ecclesia ("Called out Ones," Church).

I thank you, Holy Father, for removing all the curses that have come into my life and nation due to our belief in the doctrines of faith stated in the Council of Nicaea, concerning the Jews and the Jewish foundations of the faith. I beg you with thanksgiving to pour out your great mercy and forgiveness over myself, my family, and nation. As a result of this, I commit myself to walk in Truth as You reveal it to me in love, with all my fellow relatives; especially my spiritual parents who are the Jewish people according to Genesis 12:1-3. In Yeshua's name I pray; amen!

APPENDIX

EXTRA INFORMATION

Why is it so urgent to bring this information?
1. Yahveh is a Holy God.
2. Anti-Semitism is rising to alarming proportions throughout the world.
3. Satan wants to destroy Israel by means of the Palestinian Issue.
4. Archbishop Dominiquae was visited by the Lord in Chile when He showed her that after 2,000 years of the gospel, there was not one nation that He could call a "Sheep Nation." (See Matthew 25:32.)
5. Satan wants to destroy all the nations by influencing them to hate God's Torah (Laws and precepts) and to hate the Jewish people and the State of Israel. (See Isaiah 34, Obadiah, Zechariah 12, Psalms 83.)
6. The church is supposed to disciple Nations. (See Matthew 28:19.)

7. The church has to change and return to the Jewish/biblical roots and retrieve the gospel that the Jewish Apostles preached. Prophecy from Lance Lambert:

> "My anger is stirred up, says the Lord, against the nations for they are dividing My land and seeking to destroy my heritage. My furious anger is like a boiling cauldron against those powerful states that have produced such strategies and who by pressure and manipulation are seeking to implement them. Now, I will become their enemy, says the Lord, and I will judge them with natural disasters, by physical catastrophes, by fire, by flood, by earthquakes, and by eruptions. I will touch the seas, the atmosphere, the earth and all that is within them. Moreover, I will touch them where it will hurt them the most for I will touch their power and the foundations of affluence and prosperity. I will smash their prosperous economies, says the Lord. And I will overturn, and overturn, and overturn that they may know that I am the Lord."

Michael McGarry, *The Holocaust and the Christian World* by Ritner, Smith & Steinfeldt:

> Many Christians when confronted with the Shoa (Nazi Holocaust), gaze on it as if some aliens landed on the earth, took the name 'Nazi' and proceeded to torture and kill Jews. They regard the perpetrators of these monstrous acts as from another planet, as people that otherwise did not hug their children, weep at the death of a parent, bleed when they were wounded – in other words, non-human creatures without a conscience, automatons of some mad and evil creator. But the Shoa (Holocaust) is not the story about a group of alien people, rather about human beings. And they, we must admit, were primarily Christians, from the great Lutheran and Cath-

olic tradition. Somehow they had lost that which made them followers of Jesus or they had chosen to suppress it in their horrid pursuit of killing Jews.

The following illustration will explain why Christianity was "the womb" of the Spanish Inquisition, the Crusades, and the Nazi Holocaust. Yahveh-God is looking to the church for repentance to influence the nations and fulfill the mandate of Matthew 28:19, "Go and make disciples of all nations."

Two Weddings and One Divorce

The first and original church was married to a Jewish Husband by the name of Yeshua the Messiah and into His family, the Jewish people. (See Ephesians 2:14 and Romans 11.) The Wedding Ceremony took place in Jerusalem. It was ratified and sealed by the spilling of the Blood of the Husband and by the breaking of His body. (See Luke 22:15–20.) The time of this marriage was the holy biblical Feast of Passover. The fruit of this awesome wedding was thousands and thousands of people, both Jews and Gentiles saved and healed. Even the shadow of this holy bride healed the sick, as signs and wonders and miracles followed her wherever she went in the name of her Husband Yeshua.

This marriage led the wife into much suffering. Many in the world did not love her Husband and tried to kill her by persecuting her and even throwing her to the lions during the Roman Empire's reign of terror. Those were hard years. After many years of suffering, Yeshua's wife had become weary. He had gone to prepare a place for her and had not come back yet.

She started to get tired of her lifestyle as an outcast, persecuted, and hunted at every corner. She longed for peace at any price. She longed for the warm embrace of a Husband who would provide her with peace and security here on this earth. At her weakest point, an earthly king appeared. (See Matthew 10:34, John 14:27, Jeremiah 8:11.)

This earthly king was influential and powerful by worldly standards. He could stop the killing and persecution against her. He could give her the security she longed for: if only she would agree to divorce this Jewish Husband of hers and utterly separate from His family Israel, and from that Book that she treasured so much – where He had left her all of His instructions and the family legacy of God's Word.

This powerful king seemed to be a spiritual man. He claimed that her Jewish Husband had appeared to him in a dream and had given him the crown of the Roman Empire. His deceptive charm and appealing manners managed to attract the very weary bride of Messiah, but not all were deceived. There was a portion of the bride/church/Ecclesia that was not fooled by the charms of this deceitful king. These were the Messianic Jews of the time.

They were too rooted in the writings of the Holy Book and the ancient Hebrew Scriptures to be deceived. But the vast majority of the believers at that time were Gentiles, and they did not want any more suffering on behalf of the Book, its Author, or His Family.

They wanted freedom and peace at all cost.

The powerful Constantine sang the song of peace and safety and prepared a bed of roses. The Gentile portion of the church slept with him, falling into violent adultery and wounding the heart of her heavenly Jewish Husband. To appease the conscience of this adulterous church, Constantine decided to legalize this unholy union in the year 325 AD through a wedding ceremony called the Council of Nicaea and drawing up an ungodly and illegal marriage contract called *the Nicene Creed*.

He used his worldly power to draw all the Gentile church fathers, which for the most part were already anti-Semitic and hated their Jewish roots. These church fathers were to be witnesses of this horrendous divorce and the adulterous new marriage between the predominantly Gentile church and another Jesus, a product of Constantine's creation.

This alternative Savior came with another family, another book (totally disconnected from the ancient Hebrew writings,) other customs, laws, festivals, traditions, and ways of measuring time.

Knowing that his brand-new wife was accustomed to worshipping God, he organized for her a god that would suit her perfectly by not demanding any holiness from her. He presented a god of peace that was lenient towards a mixture of paganism and holiness: an all-inclusive god, who accepted all traditions and blended them into one.

Now Passover and First Fruits, which was the festival of Yeshua's Resurrection, would become the Feast of Ishtar, the goddess of fertility, or Easter with bunny rabbits and Easter eggs. (At that time eggs were dipped in the blood of the babies sacrificed to the goddess, thus the tradition of painting the eggs.)

Now the day of worship would change from Shabbat to Sunday to eternalize the sun god who for now would be called Jesus – yet it was another Jesus and certainly not Yeshua–the Jewish Messiah.

Then the day of the Winter Solstice of witchcraft, called Saturnalia or Paganalia, celebrated on the 25th of December in the Roman Empire, was to acquire the name Christmas and would celebrate the birth of this false Messiah. For the true Messiah was born during the holy biblical Feast of Tabernacles and followed the Hebrew biblical calendar, not the Roman one. (See Daniel 7:25–27, Jeremiah 10:2–4 about the Christmas tree.)

The ancient Holy Book of the Hebrew Scriptures was to become obsolete, and its Laws were done away. Instead, Constantine compiled the apostolic writings, the letters of Paul and others into a new holy book and called it the New Testament. He gave this holy book his own perverse interpretation, completely divorced from the foundational Hebrew writings whom he and his followers called the "Old Testament" (Matthew 5:17–21.)

In rejecting their custom, we may transmit to our descendants the legitimate way of celebrating Easter... We ought not therefore to have anything in common with the Jew, for the Savior has shown us another way; our worship following a more legitimate and more convenient course (the order of the days of the week); And consequently, in unanimously adopting this mode, we desire dearest brethren to separate ourselves from the detestable company of the Jew. (Excerpt from *The Nicene Creed*, year 325, found in Eusebius, Vita Const. Lib III 18–20)

This creed and its instructions are still followed by most Christians today with the celebration of Easter, Christmas, Sunday (replacing Shabbat), and the rejection of the Laws of God.

Indeed, a new religion had been born. It had a Gentile god by the name of Jesus Christ; an apostle by the name of Constantine; a new book by the name of the New Testament (although compiled from the apostolic writings, which are completely Yah-inspired, it was deceitfully interpreted through gentile eyes and gentile theologians); new traditions, and unholy festivals such as Easter, Christmas, Sunday, and Halloween.

Most importantly... No Jews... No, not even the Messiah.

What has been the Fruit of this Adulterous Marriage?

"Either make the tree good and its fruit good, or else make the tree bad and its fruit bad; for a tree is known by its fruit."

Matthew 12:33

The fruit of the first holy matrimony were salvations and healings.

The fruit of this ungodly and *pagan* marriage was forced conversions and *murder*, yes, even mass destructions of the family of Yeshua the Messiah, (the true Husband), in the name of the false Jesus Christ god created by Constantine.

A god who, according to Constantine in the Nicene Creed, had shown us another way. What was that way? It is a way of jealousy, hatred, killing, destruction, and *Lawlessness*. Horrendous Christian events such as pogroms, the holy Inquisition, and the Holocaust, have taken place since this ungodly 4th century marriage and the creation of this false religion.

The hatred conveyed in the Nicene Creed against the Jews and anything Jewish, including the Torah and the Old Testament, has continued through the great Protestant Reformation of the 16th century, and it still influences Christians today.

The following excerpt is from *Our Hands are Stained with Blood* by Michael Brown, as he quotes directly from Martin Luther's writings. Luther wrote this after he was frustrated from trying to evangelize the Jews and when he was old and sick:

> What shall we Christians do with this damned rejected race of Jews? First, their synagogues should be set on fire. Secondly, their homes should likewise be broken down and destroyed. Thirdly, they should be deprived of their prayer books and Talmud's. Fourthly, their rabbis must be forbidden under threat of death to teach anymore. Fifthly, passports and traveling privileges should be absolutely forbidden to the Jews…To sum up dear princes and nobles, who have Jews in your domains, if this advice of mine does not suit you, then find a better one. So that you and we may all be free of this insufferable, devilish burden – the Jews.

Hitler followed Luther's instructions meticulously and quoted him while doing so. The fruit? Over six million Jews exterminated in horrendous death camps and gas chambers, and many survivors scarred for life.

Prophetic Altar Call

"After two days He will revive us; on the third day He will raise us up, that we may live in His sight. Let us know; let us pursue the knowledge of Yahveh. His going forth is established as the morning; He will come to us like the rain, like the latter and former rain to the earth."

Hosea 6:2–3

The Third Day is upon us, the Third Millennium, and this is the Father's call to His Third Day church:

Come, let us return to Yeshua, to our Jewish Messiah, His Jewish Family, and His ancient Hebrew Scriptures. Come, let us reinterpret the New Testament through the eyes of the Holy Scriptures. Let us separate ourselves from our pagan husband, Constantine, and his false Jesus and let us go back to the *true* Messiah Yeshua, to His Father's Laws and precepts, to true divine holy grace, to *true* love and holiness. Let us return to Jerusalem, and let us be made whole from centuries of adultery and paganism, as we go back to the original apostolic Jewish roots of our faith.

In Yeshua's love and brokenness,
Rabbi Baruch & Archbishop Dominiquae Bierman
Kad-Esh MAP Ministries & the United Nations for Israel

Other Books by Archbishop Dr. Dominiquae Bierman

Order now online: www.kad-esh.org/shop/

The MAP Revolution (Free E-Book)
Find Out Why Revival Does Not Come... Yet!

The Identity Theft
The Return of the 1st Century Messiah

The Healing Power of the Roots
It's a Matter of Life or Death!

Grafted In
The Return to Greatness

Sheep Nations
It's Time to Take the Nations!

Restoring the Glory: The Original Way
The Ancient Paths Rediscovered

Stormy Weather
Judgment Has Already Begun, Revival is Knocking at the Door

The Bible Cure for Africa and the Nations
The Key to the Restoration of All Africa

The Key of Abraham
The Blessing or the Curse?

Yes!
The Dramatic Salvation of Archbishop Dr. Dominiquae Bierman

Eradicating the Cancer of Religion
Hint: All People Have It

Restoration of Holy Giving
Releasing the True 1,000 Fold Blessing

Vision Negev
The Awesome Restoration of the Sephardic Jews

Defeating Depression
This Book is a Kiss from Heaven

From Sickology to a Healthy Logic
The Product of 18 Years Walking Through Psychiatric Hospitals

ATG: Addicts Turning to God
The Biblical Way to Handle Addicts and Addictions

The Woman Factor by Rabbi Baruch Bierman
Freedom From Womanphobia

The Revival of the Third Day (Free E-Book)
The Return to Yeshua the Jewish Messiah

Also Available

Music Albums
www.kad-esh.org/shop/
The Key of Abraham
Abba Shebashamayim
Uru
Retorno

Get Equipped & Partner with Us

Global Revival MAP (GRM) Israeli Bible School
Take the most comprehensive video Bible school online that focuses on dismantling replacement theology.
For more information or to order, please contact us:
www.grmbibleschool.com
grm@dominiquaebierman.com

United Nations for Israel Movement
We invite you to join us as a member and partner with $25 a month, which supports the advancing of this End time vision that will bring true unity to the body of the Messiah. We will see the One New Man form, witness the restoration of Israel, and take part in the birthing of Sheep Nations. Today is an exciting time to be serving Him!
www.unitednationsforisrael.org
info@unitednationsforisrael.org

Global Re-Education Initiative (GRI) Against Anti-Semitism
Discover the Jewish identity of the Messiah and defeat Christian anti-Semitism with this online video course to see revival in your nation!
www.against-antisemitism.com
info@against-antisemitism.com

Join Our Annual Israel Tours
Travel through the Holy Land and watch the Hebrew Holy Scriptures come alive.
www.kad-esh.org/tours-and-events/

To Send Offerings to Support our Work
Your help keeps this mission of restoration going far and wide.
www.kad-esh.org/donations

CONTACT US

Archbishop Dr. Dominiquae & Rabbi Baruch Bierman
Kad-Esh MAP Ministries | www.kad-esh.org | info@kad-esh.org
United Nations for Israel | www.unitednationsforisrael.org
Zions Gospel Press | shalom@zionsgospel.com
52 Tuscan Way, Ste 202-412, 32092 St. Augustine Florida, USA
+1-972-301-7087

www.ingramcontent.com/pod-product-compliance
Lightning Source LLC
Chambersburg PA
CBHW021431070526
44577CB00001B/161